Jokes For GrandParents
(To Tell Their GrandKids)™

Trademark Information:
Downside Up™, Downside Up Have Fun and
Enjoy Life™, and Tezzy the Turtle and Design™
are trademarks of Downside Up LLC.

Author Bohdan D. Shandor
Bonita Springs, Florida
www.downsideupjokes.com

Ordering Information:
For details, contact info.dujokes@gmail.com

ISBN: 978-1-956877-00-7 (Print Edition)
ISBN: 978-1-956877-01-4 (eBook Edition)

Printed in the United States of America
First Edition

PREFACE

I am sure everyone who has ever written a Book thinks his or her Book is special and I certainly hope you'll find this *Jokes For GrandParents (That They Can Tell Their GrandKids*™ to be special for you and your family. But, the truth is, what makes this *Joke Book for GrandParents* very special is how it came to be written.

I have a grandson named Mattias, who we call "Macho." One day, not too long ago when Macho was 5 years old he came to me, while I was watching TV, with a very serious look on his face. I didn't notice him at first but when I did I saw he was thinking about what he was going to say. After thinking long and hard, he blurted out, "Didi, can you do me a favor?" He was visibly relieved he had gotten it all out. "A really BIG favor?"

"Sure, Macho" I replied, no longer caring about the TV but more curious about what he would ask of me. "Of course, I'd be happy to, what can I do?"

Macho was now totally focused, "Well, Didi, can you teach me to tell a joke." I actually had to repeat what he had just said for it to sink in. To be sure I had it right, I responded, "You want me to teach you how to tell a joke?"

"Aha," he answered.

"OK, but why are you asking me of all people?" I was very curious.

Hesitatingly he explained, "Well, Didi... I saw when you...uh... tell a joke ...uh people listen and...uh... what's good is they laugh...out loud! That's good when people laugh cause people like your jokes, Didi." I couldn't help but hug

1

him real hard and whisper in his ear, "Of course I can help." He was happy and smiling when I next asked, "But, you know, Macho, to tell a joke you have to have material, do you have any material." All of a sudden his face grew serious again and he replied, "Didi, that's the whole problem! I don't have any 'madderial' or any stuff like that. I don't have any and I don't know where to find any 'madderial' cause, you know, I don't read yet."

And that's when my daughter, Tina, overhearing the whole exchange said, "Dad, why don't you write a joke book for grandparents to tell their grandkids so they can both have fun." I thought for a moment and said, "Macho, don't worry, Mama's got a great idea- I'm going to write a book with a lot of jokes for you to tell and we can practice telling jokes together." Instantly happy, he asked, "And, other Didis can tell jokes too?"

"Yeah, that's right!" I replied.

From this beginning came a book which is intended to be more than just jokes but an interactive book for grandparents and grandchildren, parents and their children to read together, laugh together and spend time together doing things that are fun. This has become even more important in our digital age.

In various places in the book, we offer suggestions about coloring in certain black and white illustrations and also offer questions and topics to discuss with the child. We sincerely hope that through this casual interaction your child learns from you as the grandparent or parent; just as you, the grandparent or parent, learn more about your grandchild or child. And, as they say in Hollywood, "The Rest is History......."

ACKNOWLEDGMENTS

You don't usually find Acknowledgments in Joke Books but this is a *very special Joke Book*. So, we have Acknowledgments.

The first person I would like to thank and acknowledge for her tremendous contribution in making this book a reality is my partner in the DOWNSIDE UP™ Series of Joke Books, OLGA MEDYUKH. Olga and I got acquainted when I was head of a non-for-profit organization and she joined as a new member. Our first meeting was at a Starbucks off of I-75 in Florida, which finally evicted us into their parking lot because of early closing due to COVID-19. Olga and her husband Denis have a beautiful family with three girls, Victoria, Katherine and Maria and reside in Aventura, Florida. The experience of working with Olga has been especially important to the development of the book as an educational tool as we have compared parenting ideas, experiences and learning activities that transcend generational differences.

My success in publishing this book and in life would not have been possible without the love and support of my beautiful wife, MARIE SHANDOR, who is grandmother to our four wonderful grandchildren, Stefan, Mattias, Rafael and Colette.

Of course, a great big THANK YOU goes out to my daughter Tina, who was the initiator of the idea for the book and without whose encouragement this first Book may not have happened; and, her three sons Stefan and Mattias, who were both early contributors and very tough reviewers- more about that later. And, Rafa who was too little to contribute other than a very special way- just looking at him makes me smile.

My son, Alex, deserves a big THANK YOU for serving as the Editor of the book at an early stage and offering some important insights into humor. As a child, he was perhaps the youngest fan of *Seinfeld* and I believe learned much about comedy from the very popular TV program.

Many of the jokes in this book were written by me; but, most were obtained from kids who I talked to about the book. Once I told them what I was doing in writing the joke book they became eager contributors and couldn't wait to tell me their favorite jokes. I listened to hours of jokes and enjoyed every one of them. I thank them from the bottom of my heart and now I take great pleasure in sharing some of these jokes with you!

I also relied upon a select group of young reviewers who saw the jokes before publication and actually graded them. In one case, the creative young reviewers actually assigned numbers from 1 to 10, as one of them said, "like the Olympics" and then held up their scores after I told them each joke. Yes, there were some "2's and 3's" that hopefully got edited out-- with the "9's and 10's" staying in. I thank each and every one of my stalwart reviewers.

These young joke tellers and joke reviewers are the real SUPERSTARS of this book and to them I extend the BIGGEST of THANK YOU's!

Here are their names (in alphabetical order): *Blake M., Katherine S., Maddie E., Maria S., Mattias K., Max E., Max M., Olivia M., Peter J., Raquel S., Stacy T., Stefan K., and Victoria S.*

What did the turtle say when it ended up upside down?

Get my Downside UP !

Can you color Tezzy™ the Downside Up Turtle?

What do you call
two bananas?

A slippery pair.

What sits at the bottom of the ocean and twitches?

A nervous wreck.

✎ *Can you draw your own shipwreck?*

Knock ! Knock !

Q: Who's there?

A: Sez

Q: Sez who?

A: Says me that's who!

How do fleas get from
one town to the next?

By itch-hiking.

Where do sheep go on vacation?

The Baaa-hamas.

How do you cure a sick bird?

With tweet-ment.

✎ *Think of the different colors to color the bird.*

What do cats eat for breakfast?

Mice Crispies.

What do you like for breakfast?

If a chicken gets hit by a Ferrari while crossing the street, what do you have?

Chicken-ala-Ferrari.

Why did the math book look so confused?

Because it had a lot of problems.

What do you call a can
opener that doesn't work?

A can't opener.

Knock ! Knock !

Q:Who's there?

A: Annie

Q: Annie who?

A: Annie body going to open the door?

What do you call a
missing parrot?

A polygon.

Why was the cat sent to
investigate a plane crash?

Because it was a cat-astrophe.

What do you call a parrot wearing a raincoat?

Polly unsaturated.

Can you color in the parrot and umbrella?

What do you call a monkey if you take away his bananas?

Furious George!

How would you draw George?

Did you hear about the crook
who stole a calendar?

He got twelve months.

What do you call a sleeping bull?

A bull dozer.

How do you stop a bull from charging?

Cancel its credit cards.

What do you call an
old snowman?

Why do people tell actors
to break a leg?

Because every play has a cast.

What do you call a bear with no teeth?

A Gummy Bear.

Why shouldn't you write
with a broken pencil?

Because it's pointless.

Why was the baby ant so confused?

Because all of its uncles were ants.

Knock ! Knock !

Q: Who's there?

A: Macaroon

Q: Macaroon who?

A: See you soon, Macaroon!

Did you hear about the actress
who fell through the floor?

She was just going
through a stage.

Why does a chicken coup
have two doors?

Because if it had four doors it
would be a chicken sedan.

Why didn't the Duck cross the road?

Because a car came along and he quacked up.

Why are ghosts such bad liars?

Because you can see
right through them.

What kind of snake likes to build things?

A Boa Constructor.

Why did the laptop get glasses?

To improve its web sight.

Knock ! Knock !

Q: Who's there?

A: Crocodile

Q: Crocodile who?

A: In a while crocodile. I have to open the door !

What do you call a professional cheese maker who lives alone?

Pro-vo-lone.

What do you get when a banana becomes a gymnast?

A Banana Split.

What do you call a boomerang that won't come back?

A stick.

✎ *Can you draw what a boomerang looks like?*

What do you call a
schizophrenic boomerang that
always comes back fast?

A pain in the neck.

Why is it not a good idea to eat a clock?

Because it's very time consuming.

 *Can you draw a clock?*

What do you call it when you have your granny on speed dial?

Insta-Gran.

Why was the bed
wearing a disguise?

Because it was undercover.

How does a gourmet Chef make an egg roll?

She pushes it.

Can you draw what you would look like as a gourmet chef?

Daddy, I have a question.

Ok, son what is it?

How do you know when you've run out of invisible ink?

What do you call a pig that knows karate?

A pork chop.

Why did the tortoise always keep a pin in her pocket when racing cars?

To better handle the hare pin turns.

Why do ducks fly south for the winter?

Because it's too far to walk.

Why don't architects
play football?

Because they each have
their own plans.

What's the best snack to eat during a horror movie?

I-scream!

✎ Can you name six different flavors of ice cream?

Why do railroad engineers
make good race car drivers?

Because they know how
to stay on track.

Why was #6 scared of #7 ?
Because 7 ate 9 !

✎ *Color in the numbers above.*

Where do cows go for entertainment?

The mooo-vees.

What is your favorite movie?

What do you get when you put a bullet proof vest on an alligator?

An investigator.

What did one wall tell the other wall?

Let's meet at the corner.

**What day do chickens
go into hiding?**

Fry-day!

Where do polar bears keep their money?

In Snow Banks.

✎ *Color in the picture above.*

A bear walks into a cafe
and says, "Give me a cola
and ....lemon."

The waiter asks, "why
the big pause?"

The bear says, "I don't know
I was born with them."

Can you draw a bear's paw print?

What do you call a rabbit that has fleas?

Bugs bunny !

What is a snake's favorite subject in school?

Hisssssss tory!

✎ *Color the picture above.*

What species of snake
never orders desert?

A Pie-thon.

What starts with an "e" ends with an "e" and has only one letter in it?

Envelope.

✎ *Draw an envelope and put your address on it.*

Did you hear about the new restaurant opening on the Moon?

Great menu but no atmosphere.

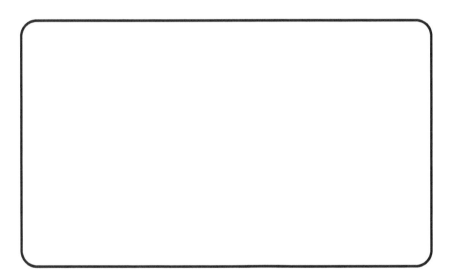

🖎 *Can you draw a restaurant on the moon?*

What's the scariest building in New York City?

The Vampire State Building!

Do you know how many floors the Empire State Building has?

What do you call a Bee that comes from America?

USB

Do you know what a USB is used for?
Hint: it saves information stored on a computer.

What do you call a magic dog?

A Labracadabrador!

✎ What color do you think a labracadabrador is?

What do you call an ant that won't go away?

Perman-ant.

 *Can you name two types of ants?*

Why didn't the skeleton go to the prom?

Because he had no-body to dance with.

What hurts most when you fall?

The ground coming
up to meet you.

 *Do you know what causes things to fall?*

How do you learn to make the best banana splits?

Go to Sundae School.

What would you put on your best banana split?
Don't forget the whip cream!

What do you call a dog that likes to swim with polar bears?

A pup-sicle.

 *What's your favorite popsicle flavor?*

Knock ! Knock !

Q: Who's there?

A: Toad

Q: Toad who?

A: I toad you so!

What do you call someone who's afraid of Santa?

Claus-tro-pho-bic.

What did one strawberry tell the other strawberry?

You sure got us in a jam.

✐ Color in the strawberries.

What do you call a tree
that has a lot of angles?

A ge-ome-tree.

What animal is much smarter
than a talking parrot?

A spelling Bee.

Why did the golfer wear
two pairs of pants?

In case he got a hole in one.

Why did the baby Hippopotamus change his name when he got older?

Because H-I-P-P-O-P-O-T-A-M-U-S was too hard to spell.

What do you call a dog in the winter?

A chilli dog.

What do you like to put on your hot dog?

What do you call a Penguin in the middle of the desert?

Lost!

Why do some fish live in saltwater?

Because pepper makes them sneeze.

 *Can you name three other spices or seasonings?*

What's a librarian's favorite vegetable?

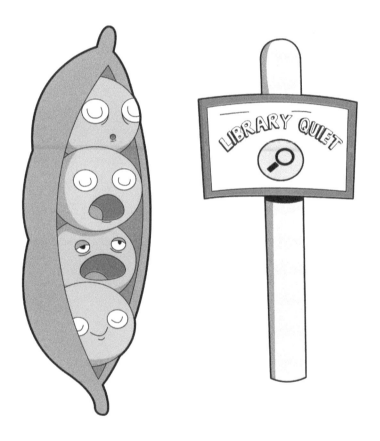

Quiet Peas.

If a seagull flies over the sea, what flies over the bay?

A bagel.

 *What other birds can you name?*

Why don't leopards like to rob banks?

Because they always get spotted?

✍ What other animal has spots?

What did one mackerel fish say when he saw his friend?

Holy mackerel !

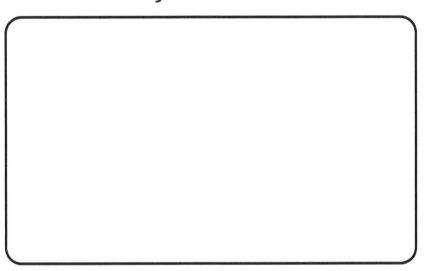

✎ Can you draw a mackerel fish?

What did one flounder
say to the other flounder
when he saw a shark?

SHARK !

What did the leopard say
to her friend when she
stepped out of the shower?

You look spotless.

What animal really likes rain?

A reindeer.

What animal is always laying around?

A Lie-on.

Can you draw a lion?

Why did the rocket scientist install a knocker on her front door?

Because she wanted to win the No-Bell Prize.

What street do lions like to drive on the most?

MANE Street.

*Do you know what your address is?*

What do you call a duck that says oink, oink?

A very confused duck.

Why is Cinderella so bad at soccer?

Because she always runs away from the ball.

 *What is your favorite sport?*

What is black and white and red all over?

A penguin with a sunburn.

Why did the bicycle fall over?

Because it was two tired!

Why did the thoroughbred racehorse never become an opera singer?

Because she got hoarse.

Why was the picture
sent to prison?

Because it was framed.

Why was the refrigerator jealous of the freezer?

Because he was a lot cooler.

Why was one mountain taller than the other mountain?

Because it went to high school.

 *Can you name a mountain?*

Why wasn't the owl worried about winter coming?

Because he didn't give a hoot.

What kind of fish loves extra candles on its birthday cake?

A Blowfish.

Color in the fish and cake above.

Knock ! Knock !

Q: Who's there?

A: Felix

Q: Felix who?

A: I Feel-ix-Austed, let me in!

What has four wheels and flies?
A garbage truck.

✎ *Can you draw what a garbage truck would look like?*

**What did the ocean say
when it met the beach?**

It didn't say anything – it waved.

Coming Soon...

Jokes for Retirees and Seniors
(That You May Not Want To Tell The Boss)

OLGA MEDYUKH grew up in New York City. She wears many hats and fills many shoes as a mother of three wonderful girls, ages 5, 8 and 11; as an attorney; and, now as a Co-Founder and Head of Creative Production for DOWNSIDE UP LLC.

Olga brings a personal and generational perspective that adds to a better understanding of what it takes today to coax developing children away from the habitual staring at video screens. Working together and bridging the generational differences, Olga and the Author worked to further the learning experience beyond reading, discussion and telling jokes. Olga's creative input and use of "action prompts," be it drawing or answering fun questions, add teaching moments to the interactive experience between grandparents, parents and children.

Her tenacity, perseverance and willingness to take on new challenges has been a major factor in the successful introduction of Jokes for GrandParents (To Tell Their GrandKids)™ and no doubt will be important to the introduction of future books by DOWNSIDE UP LLC.

BOHDAN D. SHANDOR was born and raised in Paterson, New Jersey, where he learned early on that survival in a tough city meant knowing how to run fast, hide quickly and be a diplomat-- the key to which is often humor. "Usually, you don't get punched as hard if the other guy is smiling or laughing".

After graduating from The Wharton School and receiving post-graduate degrees in business and law from New York University, Bohdan's work in Mergers & Acquisitions took him around the world where getting deals done was again dependent on diplomacy, working with people and where a sense of humor and a smile were always an asset.

What led to the creation of the Downside Up™ Series of Joke Books was Bohdan's grandsons, ages 5 and 7; who inspired him to write a joke book that children, parents and especially grandparents can enjoy with their grandchildren.

We hope this Downside Up™ Joke Book brings you an abundance of joy, happiness and laughter with your grandchildren, children and families. Also, be on the lookout for future Downside Up™ Joke Books that add a touch of humor to retirement, divorce, marriage, parenting and other lifetime events.

Visit us at:
www.downsideupjokes.com

Milton Keynes UK
Ingram Content Group UK Ltd.
UKHW020823030923
427910UK00007B/147

9 781956 877007